GET THE EDGE!
Networking 1-on-1

Secrets of a networking superstar

Author:
Bev Edgerton

Networking1on1.com
bevedge@aol.com
309 826-2101

Literary Consultant: Vikki Baptiste

Networking 1-on-1

Networking 1-on-1 1
Forword 2
Introduction 4
What is networking? 4
What keeps us from networking? 5
Networking: Where to start 6
The Story of Mr. Jones 8
Ready to follow Mr. Jones' example? Let's network! 19
The heart of networking 23
Reasons for networking properly 24
How do you know where to network? 25
Does networking bring instant results? 26
How do you ask for business? 27
The importance of the follow-up 28
How do you ask for referrals? 29
Do you network *everywhere* you go? 30
How do you present yourself? 31
Practice "Safe Networking"! 32
But Bev. I'm an introvert, can you help me? 32
Networking etiquette 35
Building on the Relationship 38
Networking 1-on-1 For Groups 41
Need an icebreaker? 43
Bonus Chapter Networking 1-on-1 for senior citizens .. 45
Why is networking important to nursing home
residents? 45
Seminars 47
Networking in alternative situations 49
Networking Tools 50
Business Cards 50
Print and Vehicle Advertising 51
Billboards 53
Testimonials 53

Foreword!

Networking 1 on 1 is a book with long term life experience woven into its pages. Those of us who have been in business for a while know that business growth is rarely the result of one strategy or tactic. It's a lot of small things that guide a business to success. This book teaches people how to combine business concepts with new marketing tools and strategies. The result is an efficient and effective process to develop a plan - a roadmap for growth and success for your business.

The book presents marketing in an entirely new light. It highlights some of the problems in sales and marketing that have persisted for decades...and how to fix them. It will show individuals how to organize around customers instead of products and most importantly, how to build relationships.

This book was written for anyone who is looking for something new in marketing. New and experienced entrepreneurs, marketers and CEO's will find this book full of fresh new ideas, including how to measure marketing and how to use social media to build customer relationships. Bev teaches you a real-time planning process that keeps pace with change. It's a flexible process, so you create a plan that is an operational document to help the entire business execute strategy and continuously improve.

I know from experience that a healthy, thriving culture is essential to the foundation of every successful business. Companies that foster a thriving culture create a strong, internal brand and that is the secret to creating a powerful brand. This book will certainly show you how to create happy, engaged business associates and build relationships.

Julie Dobski, Co-Owner
Little Jewels Learning Center
McLean Area McDonald's

Introduction

This book does not have all of the answers for everyone. It does have many answers for some. And this book will show you how to network effectively.

Bev Edgerton wrote the Book on networking!

Personally, I have personal and business Facebook pages. I do some Twitter and LinkedIn, and I'm open to all social sites. Skype is becoming very popular. You can talk to a person anywhere in the world and see their face as you interact with them. Social media, cell phones, texting, email; these are all incredible social phenomena, but ...

... through any of these media, can you touch a person? Can you shake their hand, hug them, and pat them on the back or even smile at them?

Networking 1-on-1 is an option.
It will give you avenues to use to network effectively, making acquaintances and long-term business associates and even friends.

Networking is an art. It is an acquired talent. Doing it wrong is worse than not doing it at all!

What is networking?
According to Merriam-Webster, Networking is the exchange of information or services among institutions, individuals, groups, or *specifically*: the

Your Notes and Thoughts

cultivation of productive relationships for employment or business.

Networking is not just making a connection; it's making a valid connection.

What keeps us from networking?

There are a number of reasons people feel uncomfortable networking, and the most prevalent is lack of self-esteem.

Past experiences can interfere with a person's confidence level, and positive self-esteem can help you rise above any circumstances by giving you courage. Not so, in those with low self-esteem. But how do we change that? What kind of self-talk can we use to push us into a position where we can feel comfortable in a room full of strangers?

Affirmations are an excellent way to start on the journey to greater self-esteem. Replace thoughts like "I'm not as experienced as others in the room" with more positive thoughts, such as "I am a leader in my industry!" If your brain hears this positive thought more than the "I'm not good enough" thought, then it believes that thought, and your confidence will grow.

Whenever negativity creeps into your mind, counter it with a positive thought! If you can't think of anything positive based on the same subject matter, ANYTHING positive will do!

Your Notes and Thoughts

As you continue using positive thoughts to replace negative thoughts, you will find that this positive way of thinking becomes natural – your subconscious is tricked into thinking these positive thoughts are the truth. Easier said than done? It takes persistence, but you will be a more positive person if you continue this practice.

Try to train your brain not to travel back into the past and recall bad experiences. You can do this by imagining that you have achieved the goals you are striving for, and living as if your goals have been reached. Always use "I" in your affirmations. "I am living the lifestyle I dreamed about." "I am a master networker." "I am blessed with abundance."

Don't expect to change in just one day. Mastering positivity takes time and consistency. Each time a negative thought enters your mind; counter it with positivity, until it becomes second nature .If you're having problems coming up with positive affirmations on the spur of the moment, try writing them down on paper and repeating them – aloud –each morning.

Networking: Where to start

Two of the most important elements in networking are sincerity and taking a genuine interest in the

> **Here's a tip:** Oftentimes we meet many people in a short timeframe. To help you remember facts about each person, jot them down on the back of their business card.

Your Notes and Thoughts

person you are talking with. You should strive to make each encounter real and memorable, no matter how short the face-to-face time is.

Make sure the conversation centers around the person you're talking to, they are the most important person in the conversation if you make it so.

You can never network too much. But you can network in all the wrong places, so it's important to pick your most productive opportunities. During networking events it's nice to be amongst your peers but can be ineffective if that's all there is. i.e. "no realtor is going to buy a house from me, since I myself am a realtor in a room full of realtors."

One secret to networking success in business is to not focus on the sale, or the business goal. Build the relationship and it will come, just like the harvest! People like to do business with people they know, so if they never meet you, they won't know you.

Networking can become very tiresome. However, you have to keep going and going. It takes total commitment. It only works if you work it. It only works if you continue, and may eventually lead to burnout. Remember that not every occasion has to land you a large sale or contract. Sit back and relax at some socials and allow people to come to you.

Be yourself, and talk with people you know about casual things: sports, weather, family, etc. You will

Your Notes and Thoughts

> **Here's a tip:**
> Read your local newspaper and find an event that interests you, or would help you make new relationships, then attend the event. Don't reveal you are uninvited; remember the event was advertised for you.

feel refreshed and may have a new approach to your serious networking. It's like taking a mini vacation but never leaving home. Try it!

You may be comfortable networking from behind a computer screen, but it is not uncommon to feel "stuck" when you are in a person-to-person situation.

The Story of Mr. Jones

Mr. Jones just opened a new business that he has always dreamed of owning. The product he sells is something that lasts, under normal circumstances, for five years.

Mr. Smith is Mr. Jones first real customer. He loves the enthusiasm that Mr. Smith has, and makes the first purchase.

Mr. Jones loves his product. He did extensive research before opening the business, and knows that he has the best product money can buy.

Mr. Smith assures Mr. Jones that he will tell everyone he meets about this new business. Isn't that wonderful? But … how many of these people

Your Notes and Thoughts

need Mr. Jones' product? Odds are … maybe one. Odds are, Mr. Smith may forget. Odds are, Mr. Jones will need to find more customers.

Mr. Jones needs to learn how to network!

How hard is it to teach Mr. Jones how to network?

He's waiting patiently for all the referrals from Mr. Smith. But realistically, a new business owner cannot "wait" for too long.

Mr. Jones thinks that advertising should work! Now, where to advertise? He already has an expensive ad in the phone book. This was a "must". He has a fairly expensive store sign. But wonders what advertising medium will bring him the most exposure.

He tries the local newspaper. He can track this advertising with a sale item. Everybody wants a bargain! This brings him some new sales, and some new people to talk to. Now we're getting somewhere!

As part of his newspaper advertising, his customers have to fill out their name and address. He uses these details to compile a list, and sends out thank you notes. With the note, he includes another offer and asks for referrals. The offer he makes is good for 30 days, and can be used by anyone. If the customer offers this to another person, he offers

Your Notes and Thoughts

another incentive.

This builds his network of referral clients, and he is gathering personal information on each of them.

Mr. Jones still needs more customers if he's going to pay the bills!

He is laying the groundwork to become a great networker, and is doing the right things to build his business.

Mr. Jones Grows Into a Successful Business Person

Mr. Jones has tried several great advertising plans now in order to build his new business. Some have been fairly successful! The number of sales is his measure of success, but he doesn't need his sales to be too far apart. Consistency and innovation are the real "meat and potatoes". There are many places to advertise. Some are wasteful, and some keep your name in front of potential customers.

Mr. Jones realizes that his "one sale at a time" approach has got his business off to a good start; however, he still needs real, repeat customers.

How can he find them, and how can he get them to his business?

He hears of networking groups and how they are a very good source of business leads. What he must

Your Notes and Thoughts

learn is that they only work, and work well, if he is willing to make a commitment. He has to ride out the slow times, and always has to be there for the perfect referral.

How does he get the perfect referral? He has to ask for it! Networking is not just being at the group meeting. It's being direct with your needs. Most businesses do more than one thing, or do one thing in a variety of ways. Do the other members of his networking group know exactly what he can do, and how?

He can directly ask for his perfect referral more than once. Maybe someone who knows the very person he needs to know was not there, or not listening. Maybe that person just didn't catch it the first time.

So, he will further his own success if he spends quality time with networking groups, consistently ask for the perfect referral, and promote this request in a pamphlet or brochure, which he distributes.

Now, Mr. Jones is on the real road to success!

What Else Can Mr. Jones Do to
Further His Business?

To expand his networking circle, he needs to find several networking opportunities. Yes, I said several.

Your Notes and Thoughts

Opportunities include BNI (Business Networking International), Rotary and other service clubs, and, of course, the local Chamber of Commerce.

The key to all of this networking is consistency. Mr. Jones must make his presence known at every opportunity. He must participate as much as possible. If he is unable to attend a meeting or function, he can sponsor a table, or donate a raffle prize. He should be creative in the process. People who win prizes often forget where they came from, so his sponsorship or prize should include a trip to his business to pick up the prize. And the prize should also include a coupon for future business services they may need.

Mr. Jones needs to find a way to get his product in front of people with the help of these groups that he is a member of. Taking the Chamber of Commerce as an example, he could sponsor a brown bag lunch program that spotlights his business or his product. He can attend the Before or After Hours events, Power Lunches, SpeedNets and Ribbon Cuttings … showing that he supports other businesses in the community.

Most Chambers sponsor a range of activities, such as golf outings, galas, tailgating, and Ambassador program, and much more.

Mr. Jones may be shy about speaking in front of an audience, so he should practice at home, make

Your Notes and Thoughts

good bullet-point notes in large print (for reference), and keep his narrative short and concise, until he's comfortable speaking to a crowd.

If you've been keeping track how many people Mr. Jones has connected with since we started this story, your mind should be boggled! Now, for each person he gave his business card to, he should have collected one of theirs. Now what should he do? Follow up, of course!

Mr. Jones Follows Up

Follow up is a tough one. Let's see how Mr. Jones can effectively make this grow his business.

He could call all the people he has business cards for and have lunch with them in order to get to know them better. That would incur some serious expense! A better approach is to pick a "chosen few" and have a lunch date. Or even coffee. The people he picks should be his top prospects.

The real trick is that he is not spending this time to make a sale. He is purely building a relationship. The meetings should concentrate on that person's business, community activities, even personal life … how many children, dogs, cats, hobbies, etc.

Now he has some ammunition! It's what BNI calls "Givers Gain". He should have a list, a book of cards, or even mental notes. Now, what does he do?

Your Notes and Thoughts

- Ask for a sale?
- Give them his sales pitch?
- Talk about himself?

Answer: None of the above!

He has listened to information about their business, their community involvement, their family and hobbies. Now, he gives them a referral.

Mr. Jones says "You should talk to Mr. Edwards about this. He's very active in that area. Here's his business card (or phone number)" or "I know a business that would be great for you to contact!

You could refer to each other or work together on a project."

The opportunities here are endless, but the key is to give something of value. It must be specific, not a suggestion. He hears suggestions from well-meaning friends all day. Mr. Jones must have the knowledge and use all the people he has cultivated in his quest for business. What the end result should be is, this person remembers and either does business with Mr. Jones, or gives a glowing referral to someone else. The person he told this individual could help him appreciates the connection and does the same for Mr. Jones.

Follow up, you will remember, is crucial. Follow up is not just a "thank you" card. It's an ongoing process. Read that again. Follow up is an ongoing

Your Notes and Thoughts

process. Everyone enjoys a "thank you" note or call. Then that person fades away. A mailing list is essential. The mailout can be monthly, or quarterly, but it is a must. The trick here is that it needs to be personalized. You may think that is difficult. It is, but it can be simplified.

Add a personal note to a few mailers each time. Keep a check mark by the name on your list, and don't duplicate. Be aware of everything that happens in the community. Send an article to a person you know would be interested, or call them. Know what your sphere is interested in doing. When those lunches/coffees/networking meetings are over, make notes by the name on the business cards.

Never underestimate the personal touch!

Reaping the Benefits of Your Labor

Follow up is so diverse. There is not room in this book to cover all the ins and outs, but a few very good hints will help a person invent their own avenues.

In the follow up, always be professional. You have to look professional, sound professional and act professional. At the same time, you have to be a close personal friend. Remember the notes about the client's family, hobbies, dogs, kids, etc.? Now is a good time to insert those tidbits. They really make

Your Notes and Thoughts

you look good! Wow! You remembered that? It may be only a look of pride, but you have made a deeper impression. How could this person ever say anything negative about you to anyone?

A buddy system is also a great trick. Either have someone you now know very well at an event or meeting to hand your client over to, to give them more of an opportunity to meet more people, and free you. This could be an employee, networking friend, or, even better, a person you are helping or mentoring. What a great opportunity to teach, endear yourself, and do something for someone just like someone had done for you. We never forget "Giver's Gain" There is no better principle in business or life.

All this meeting of people has many benefits. One thing can make a huge influence on a person's business. It is making yourself a powerful resource for others. If you can be known as the person who can always recommend the right person for a need, your value grows. You now have a full scope of business people that you have talked to, got their cards, and followed up on. You can judge their character and know if they are good referrals.

Never give a referral to anyone unless you have confidence and knowledge that they are qualified, honest and reliable. It can hurt your credibility more than you know if you get a reputation for giving bad referrals.

Your Notes and Thoughts

You can add many scenarios to the ones above. Anywhere you are is a great place to network! (Not necessarily at Church, that is a no-no! If someone asks for your card or a referral, make arrangements to talk later.)

Every business and job is different. Mr. Jones has come a long way. He has to settle into a niche. He needs to take the most productive avenues and concentrate on them. Sometimes it's only one at a time. Sometimes, several networking/advertising clubs or groups are a necessity to keep active enough to be always visible.

Summing Up Mr. Jones' Story

I've really come to like Mr. Jones. I like anyone who takes my advice and does everything I suggest. But, have I done enough for him? Actually, there's nothing that anyone else can teach him. He has to take all the processes learned here and expand on them. Now, it's time for him to be super creative. Now is the really tough time.

We have given Mr. Jones friends/clients/business acquaintances, and many tips. He utilized them just right. But, building and maintaining this empire is a full time job. He will need help. This type of involvement can wear a person down and injure their health!

So, our summary is to make sure he continues the

Your Notes and Thoughts

networking and relationships he has established.

Now he must have a partner/secretary/assistant, or whatever assistance his income will allow. He must choose this person very carefully. One suggestion is to invest in a temp service. He could start with a part-time employee. If it works out, he can hire this person. But if it doesn't, all he has to do is ask for a different person. There is no uncomfortable dismissal and no messy paperwork. He avoids all these problems. It is certainly something to consider.

It is imperative that he knows when the time is right for even a part-time person to carry some of the load. Too many owners don't feel comfortable sharing the wealth or the information. He must let go, and make the move.

Now comes the final and most difficult part. He needs to share all he knows even more than he already has. We gave him the tools and the knowledge. He could even be a motivational speaker whose only purpose is ... guess what? Giver's Gain!

Let's leave him traveling down this new and unchartered road. My money is on his success!

Your Notes and Thoughts

Ready to follow Mr. Jones' example?
Let's network!

The first objective of networking is to get to know each other.

What is your goal?

Assess your needs, and set your goal before you walk into the room. What are you trying to accomplish? Do you have a goal to meet 5 new people? Collect 5 business cards that you don't already have? Maybe you've networked with this group before and your goal is to set 5 follow up appointments.

> **Here's a tip:**
> Ask open-ended questions in networking conversations. Ask who, what, where, when, and how as opposed to those that can be answered with a simple yes or no. This form of questioning opens up the discussion and shows listeners that you are interested in them.

Whatever your goal, if it is the forefront of your mind, you can achieve it.

Are you "open" to networking?

What is your comfort level with this group? If you feel at ease you are more likely to network effectively. If this group is new to you, seek out someone who appears to be in a position of authority, and make yourself known to them. That

Your Notes and Thoughts

person could be your biggest ally; they probably know most of the attendees.

If you are at a networking event where food is available, eat first! If you try to eat, drink and network at the same time you're setting yourself up for failure.

Should someone approach you while you are eating, make sure you have your plate on a table, and your drink in your left hand. This leaves your right hand open to greet people.

Introducing yourself

You may be at an event where name tags have been supplied. If you're uncomfortable looking at people's name tags, you could simply start with a firm handshake, and say, "Hi, my name is ……" That usually prompts the other person to give you their name.

> **Here's a tip:** Find a networking accountability partner!

Say your name slowly and confidently, looking the other person in the eyes. This lets the person you are meeting know that you are sincere and interested in what they have to say.

Get the name right!

If the person you are meeting introduces himself as "Mr. Wright", then use "Mr. Wright" when addressing him. Be respectful of people's titles.

Your Notes and Thoughts

Don't be scared to ask them to repeat it if you didn't hear correctly. They would prefer to be called by their real name rather than the name you think you heard!

Keep the conversation flowing

Pauses can be uncomfortable for both parties. Break the silence by asking a question, or making a statement about yourself. Try to keep the conversation balanced by asking as many questions as you make statements. Remember, your goal is to learn as much as you can about the other person, not to raise your own importance!

Repetition is a good thing!

If you repeat something you have heard, such as "You said a moment ago that you are involved in Rotary, which meeting do you go to?" it shows that you're paying attention and that you want to learn more about the other person.

> **Here's a tip:** Write down your long-term networking goal

Pay attention

There is nothing worse than talking to a person who is not fully present. You know the person I mean – constantly scanning the room, or checking their phone. Even worse, texting while they are talking to you!

Your Notes and Thoughts

At this moment, there are only two people in the room. You, and the person you are talking to. Pay attention!

Did you meet your goal?

Did you ask for the other person's business card, or for a further meeting?

Did you explain your business and find out what the other person was looking to get out of this networking meeting?

And more importantly, can you help them directly, or refer them to someone else who can?

Don't leave the conversation without achieving your goal! Your blossoming relationship could turn into a sale or a referral. An effective question would be "Can I email you so that we can set up a time to talk about this further?"

The art of exiting gracefully

How do you leave a conversation and not leave the other person hanging? When you feel the conversation is over, a simple statement such as "It was great talking to you! I hope you enjoy the rest of your evening" will suffice.

You could also just say, "excuse me", and leave. Don't feel that you have to justify your exit. It's a networking event; everyone has to move on at

Your Notes and Thoughts

some point!

It can be painful for both parties to carry on a conversation that has obviously run its course, so don't be afraid to move on to the next person. It's not rude to leave people after just a few words have been spoken, as long as you excuse yourself politely.

If you know you are going to be seeing this person in the future, instead of just "talk to you soon", or "see you around", leave them with something more definite. But remember that if you say "I'll call you in the morning about that estimate." You'd better have their phone number and a reminder on your calendar!

You can also segue into a separation by introducing a third party. As a colleague passes you, pull them into the conversation, saying "have I introduced you to my colleague, Mike?" And feel free to add a conversation starter, such as "Mike has just come back from a social media convention in Chicago." The conversation is then focused on Mike, and you have an opportunity to move on to the next conversation.

The heart of networking

Networking is the art of developing and maintaining relationships with people. These relationships should be beneficial for your and your career, or

Your Notes and Thoughts

your business, however if you treat networking purely as a means of promoting your business, you're doing it wrong.

The heart of networking is making these relationships meaningful.

Reasons for networking properly.

If your sole goal for networking is to promote your business or service, you'll find yourself running out of prospects at a fast pace.

You will not be remembered unless you provide value. Or unless you can resolve another person's problem. Be different, and be memorable!

Here's a tip: Make sure your contacts in your address book are kept up to date!

The person you are networking with doesn't want to hear how your business is outpacing other businesses in your field. Nobody wants to hear how your service is better than your competitor, or how you won the award for selling the most policies. They want to hear how you can make their business, or their life, better for them. They want to learn the benefits your product can bring them.

The more you give to your network, the more you'll get in return.

Your Notes and Thoughts

How do you know where to network?

Any group that you belong to has natural, "inbuilt" networking. However, you won't have much luck selling insurance policies to a bunch of insurance salesmen. So, how do you increase your playing field?

Specific business networking groups, such as BNI (Business Networking International) are a great place to start. Everybody knows why you're there, so you never have to feel like you're skirting around the issue. And you know why everybody else is there. You are given the opportunity to let the other members know what your business is, and to ask for referrals. BNI is successfully run on the premise of "Givers Gain" – those who give referrals tend to receive referrals.

Many other networking opportunities exist in most communities. The Chamber of Commerce caters to those who are members, and many chambers provide at least one opportunity per month to interact with other Chamber members. Rotary, Kiwanis and other service groups also offer the opportunity to network with other business owners.

> **Here's a tip:** Rotary, Kiwanis and other special interest groups are great places to network – but only if you find them interesting! Nothing gets boring more quickly than a group that doesn't grab your attention.

Your Notes and Thoughts

Online services, such as meetup.com, allow you to search for networking groups in your area. Again, they could be industry-specific or general in nature.

Seek out other referral groups in your community. The more people you connect with, the more groups you'll find!

Play the field. You are not obliges to go to every networking event you're invited to, however, you need a way to know if that group or event is something you want to pursue in the future. So, attend every event you're invited to at least once.

One disclaimer, though. If you spend all your time networking, when is your work going to get done? Attend the meetings and evaluate them against each other. Which are the most valuable to you, and which are more like social gatherings?

Remember everyone either is a referral or knows a referral. Talk to everybody!

Does networking bring instant results?

Here's a tip: Schedule networking time in your calendar or planner

If networking brings you instant results, that's a bonus, but this is not par for the course. Networking is something you are constantly working at, something you are constantly perfecting, and it may take a few meetings to get around to the perfect moment that produces results.

Your Notes and Thoughts

The old adage states "people do business with people they know, like, and trust." And you're not going to be able to build those up in one meeting. The first few times you talk with a potential prospect should be the "getting to know you" phase. You need to "grow" the relationship, you and your prospect should like each other, and the trust will follow once you have nurtured the relationship.

How do you ask for business?

Don't.

Typically, if you ask for business, you are less likely to get it.

You've heard that you need an elevator pitch. Forget it! A pitch is a pitch is a pitch. And, to be honest, most elevator pitches sound contrived, rehearsed, and just downright boring!

Just go with what feels right. You're passionate about what you do, let that show, and you'll find you don't miss your elevator pitch one bit!

The preferred method is to listen to the other person talk about himself. Find their "point of pain" and offer a solution. And know that the solution you offer may not always involve you or your business.

Your Notes and Thoughts

As you listen to someone talk, in your mind you should be identifying their problems, or the questions they need answers to. It's considered impolite to interrupt the conversation to give your suggestion, so let them finish what they are saying. Once they have stopped talking, you are now in a position to say "I think I know how you can take care of that!" or "I know just the person to help you with that!" and then offer up your solution.

You will get much more mileage from this connection if you can give them a solution other than yourself ... at least in the beginning of the relationship.

There are instances where the perfect solution is your product or service. Your approach, in this case, should focus on the benefit of that product or service, not trying to sell it. For instance, "If you were to optimize your website, you'd find that more customers would find you online." would be preferable to "I can optimize your website for you!"

> **Here's a tip:** Create a profile of your ideal client and commit it to memory

The importance of the follow-up.

"The fortune is in the follow-up" is a phrase you'll often hear in business circles. Here's a tip: following a networking meeting where you've met someone new, make an entry on your calendar to

Your Notes and Thoughts

contact them a couple of days later. You could hand-write a note letting them know how glad you were to meet them. You could send them an email requesting clarification on one of their services, you could call and invite them for coffee ... whatever you do, just follow up.

> **Here's a tip:** With the next person you meet, commit to follow up within 24 hours

How many business cards did you receive in the last year? Two years? Three years? What did you do with them? Did you enter the email addresses in your computer? Did you enter the phone numbers in your cell phone? Did you keep a file of cards or are they scattered throughout your brief case, your desk, your purse? Do you ever make a re-connection with any of those business people?

The people who gave you these business cards are a very important part of your social network. If you didn't do any of the above, you can start at any time. Imagine how it makes someone feel if you just call and say, "I ran across your business card today. Maybe we should have coffee."

How do you ask for referrals?

Not everyone you meet will become your client. Most people you meet will have someone in mind they can refer to you. But how do you ask for that referral?

Your Notes and Thoughts

By practicing the art of networking for others (i.e. recommending businesses other than yourself), you set the precedent for people to refer clients to you.

> **Here's a tip:** Make a list of your desired referral partners. Who can you rely on?

Bear in mind that most people like to help others, and they like to be part of someone else's success. A simple strategy, such as asking the person if you can give them an extra business card to pass on to someone who may need your services, is an effective method of getting referrals.

Try to overcome any fear you may have of asking for a referral. The worst they can say is "no" … and "no" usually means "not at this time". Follow a "no" with a non-committal statement such as "Would you keep me in mind if you hear of anybody who could use my widgets?"

Do you network everywhere you go?

It may not be fair, but we are always in the spotlight. We are always networking. How we treat people is so important, especially strangers, so remember to project a positive attitude even when you don't feel like it. Think of the places you go daily: work, store, church, gas station, etc.

> **Here's a tip:** Make it a habit to send thank you cards

Your Notes and Thoughts

Everyone you meet should be a potential client, or sometimes even more important, a referral to one of your friends.

Networking everywhere you go is not as important as being courteous everywhere you go. Of course you are courteous to everyone at a networking event, but what about the grocery store? What about at a restaurant? What about driving? We all have our days of bad moods, but anyone you come in contact with is a potential client and/or friend.

Take a deep breath and remember that they will tell their friends how you reacted. And it really does take fewer muscles to smile than it does to frown!

How do you present yourself?

> **Here's a tip:** Think of an industry or career field you don't know anyone in, and make it a point to make contact with someone in that industry.

Well, let's see ... I don't feel good. My sales are way down. I'm pretty depressed about the economy. I'm even afraid to watch TV because the news is all bad! Should I go to the networking mixer tonight? Will my pity party show? Will people know?

This is where you have to pull yourself up by the bootstraps, put your best face forward and just DO IT! Not everyone in the room is at the top of their game. But you can be. Tell yourself all the good

Your Notes and Thoughts

things you have. Tell yourself everything positive in your life. Write them down if you must.

Now, armed with a new sense of assurance, go find someone who needs your positive attitude and, most of all, your friendly smile.

You are a professional and someone may be there who needs to learn how to be a professional. You can do it!

Practice "Safe Networking"!

Steer clear of potentially hazardous topics such as politics and religion. Unless, of course, you are in a political or religious situation with the intended purpose of networking.

But Bev. I'm an introvert, can you help me?

If you'd much rather network from behind the comparative safety of your computer screen, you're in for a treat when you get out into the real world!

Researching information on networking, and reading articles published by well-known speakers online is another way to gain networking skills.

Face-to-face human connections need not be scary, and can produce some amazing relationships. These are the unique bonds we make through seeing someone smile and laugh, rather than just

Your Notes and Thoughts

reading "LOL"!

Social anxiety is, however, real. So let's look at some ways of overcoming a fear of networking.

First of all, know that the words "introverted" and "shy" do NOT mean the same thing. Being introverted does not necessarily make you uncomfortable in networking situations, however, it can make you less likely to interact with others.

Be like Nike

Just do it. Your "comfort zone" is called that for a reason. It's where you feel comfortable, and comfortable does not increase your business.

T. Harv Eker says "Nobody ever died of discomfort, yet living in the name of comfort has killed more ideas, more opportunities, more actions and more growth than everything else combined. Comfort kills!"

Find a buddy

Is someone else you know attending this event? Get together ahead of time and arrive together. Tag along with the person you consider to be the life of the party, the most outgoing person you know, and you'll find yourself networking in no time.

Your Notes and Thoughts

Research!

Do you know who's going to be at the event? Find out some information about them or their business. Their company website is usually a good place to start!

Keep your goals in mind

You have a goal to introduce your business to 3 new people a week, for example. It's much easier to talk about your business to your friends than it is to a complete stranger, especially if you're a little shy.

Be you, be genuine, and make a friend before you make or ask for a referral.

Marian Wright Edelman says "Learn to be quiet enough to hear the genuine within yourself so that you can hear it in others."

Networking is an investment in your business. Treat it as a business tool, and it will help you overcome your fears.

It's all about them.

Take the focus off yourself, as I have pointed out throughout this book. It's not about you. It's about them.

Your Notes and Thoughts

Many people are introverted simply because they are uncomfortable being the subject of someone else's attention. And this is why networking is PERFECT for introverts. It isn't about you!

Find the connectors

You don't need to know all the plumbers in town. You need to know the person who knows all the plumbers in town.

It's much easier to network with ten key people than to try to find 100 people to connect with, and the bonds you create will be much stronger.

Stop referring to yourself as an introvert!

The law of attraction says you get more of what you focus on, so stop labeling yourself as an introvert!

That doesn't mean you have to label yourself an extrovert. There is middle ground here. Drop the label altogether, and put yourself on the same level playing field as the rest of the people in the room.

Networking etiquette
Arrive on time

If your networking meeting starts at 11:30am, be there at 11:20am. This shows respect for your host

> **Here's a tip:** Make sure you can relate the benefits of your product or service, not just the features!

Your Notes and Thoughts

and ensures that the meeting is not disrupted once it has started.

Start as you mean to go on

When entering someone's place of work, don't be rude or arrogant to the person welcoming you, whether that is a receptionist or an assistant. Be polite and respectful to everyone you encounter.

Be respectful of others

You are not the only person people have come to network with. Don't monopolize people's time, and know when to step away from a conversation.

Be prepared

We've talked about assessing your needs and setting your goals, and you also need to be prepared to answer questions about your business. If you are asked a question you don't know the answer to, the best answer is "Let me find out the answer and get back to you." This is not an admission of lack of knowledge. It's better to find out the right information than to give the wrong answer.

Leave the arrogance at the door

Confidence is a wonderful attribute to possess, yet it can easily spill over into arrogance when used as

Your Notes and Thoughts

a trait to help you "stand out" in a crowd. Don't be boastful, or try to "one-up" the competition. You may have been the top performer of the month, but a networking meeting is not the place to brag about your own accomplishments.

Ask questions

Ask lots of questions. The more you know about the other party, the more you will be able to benefit them. As you show interest in what they are saying, they will continue to open up more.

It's not all about you

As you listen to a person talk, you may become aware that you are unable to offer them any assistance through your business. This is the time to reach into your memory bank and find a link to someone else you have networked with. "You know, I don't think I can help you with that, however, I met Mr. Jones of Widgets Unlimited a couple of days ago, and I'm sure his x-gadget would be a perfect fit for your business! Let me give you his card."

Be comfortable, but don't lose your poise

Standing around for a couple of hours talking to others can become uncomfortable sometimes!

If you're in the middle of a long conversation, and you find yourself shifting your weight from foot to

Your Notes and Thoughts

foot, don't be afraid to suggest that you take the conversation to a table, or other alternative seating. But beware of the couch! Many a networking opportunity has been lost to the comfort of a plump cushion! Once you sink into the comfy confines of a couch, it's easy to lose your composure. Maintain an upright posture and you'll save not only your feet, but the conversation as well.

Building on the Relationship

We've covered the basics of face-to-face networking, and now – what do you do with all the information you've gathered?

Read the paper!

Do you read the newspaper every morning? Now your circle of acquaintances is building, you'll start recognizing some names in your local paper. Imagine how important these people would feel if you took the time to compliment them on the article? Something that I personally do is to cut out the article, laminate it, and send it to the person featured. In today's hurried world, not everyone takes time to preserve items like these, so I take the initiative and do it for them, mailed with a note saying "Loved the article!" or "It was great to see your face in the paper!"

People love to be recognized!

Your Notes and Thoughts

Create a mailing list

If you have a newsletter, pick up a business card and contact that person to ask if you can add them to your mailing list. NEVER add anyone to your list without their permission, that's one faux pas that many business people never consider and, many times, cannot resist. Recipients should be able to opt in, not have to opt out!

Meet for coffee

A coffee meeting is often a much more casual way to get to know your new acquaintances! Call to set up a time to meet for coffee, with an invitation such as "I enjoyed talking to you at the Chamber mixer the other night, and I'd really love to hear more about your business. Could we get together for coffee?"

When choosing a location to meet, make sure it's a reasonably quiet, relaxed venue. Nobody wants to try to converse over the sounds of a loud kitchen, or a group playing music in the corner!

Work on the relationship

Form a relationship first. When you know a person's interests and can recall the personal touches from your conversations, then business will happen naturally over time. Take an interest, not only in their business, but also in their family life.

Your Notes and Thoughts

"How's young Johnny's soccer team doing this season?" or "Tell your wife I said Happy Birthday!" This shows that you are paying attention to the person, and not just to their business. We've all heard the saying that people do business with people they know, like, and trust – this is what we are building here.

Make referrals

Keep your networking buddies in mind when you hear someone ask for a referral. "Do you know anyone who installs flooring?" may trigger a memory of someone you met at a previous event – but how easily can you find his or her details! Here's a trick – enter the information into your phone, as mentioned previously, but add a tag such as "flooring" or "carpets" because, chances are, you will remember what they do before remembering their name!

Today's smartphones have the capability of storing notes along with contact details, but if you don't have this function on your phone, simply list the person as "Carpet Dan Smith" – it makes them much easier to find in your contact list!

Ask for referrals

"Keep me in mind if you hear of anyone looking for a realtor!" or "Do you know anyone who is thinking about a new home?"

Your Notes and Thoughts

A statement and a question. Which do you think would serve you better? A statement does not require a reply, so it doesn't usually "stick" in a persons head for very long. However, if you ask for something specific, such as "Do you know of anyone who is thinking about buying or selling a home?" it requires the person to think. Of course they may not be able to give you a referral right away, but because they have spent time thinking about your question, your name is likely to come to mind when they DO hear of someone who wants to move!

Networking 1-on-1 For Groups

As I have said, there are right and wrong ways to network, and when you network with people, you want to make yourself unforgettable. When you walk into a room and see a group of people networking, what do you see? If you know some of them, your first inkling is to gravitate to them and start a conversation.

If you are a complete stranger you may feel invisible, they all look like professionals that know each other and you are the outsider.

Put yourself in that position. What do you think they are thinking? Do you feel how really professional and networking savvy they are? Do you feel they have it all together?

Your Notes and Thoughts

> **Here's a tip:** Host an event for people in your network!

There's no way to tell who these people are, so what do you do? Remember everyone is, or knows, a referral.

You take the initiative. Introduce yourself, give a card, ask for a card, read it, then ask about them and their company. What do they do? How long have they done it? Keep the conversation on them until they direct it to you.

It at all possible, write a note on the back of the card before you forget details. Drop them a handwritten note just to say how nice it was to meet them - and try to include one fact you learned.

Now, let's practice the balancing act. First, a few hints. Besides balancing a planner and/or a drink, what about your purse, ladies? Here is one way to avoid the famous balancing act. After all, you may be there to eat and drink, but meeting people should be your first priority.

So, what do you talk about? When the time comes to talk about you, you should focus on what sets you apart, what makes you unique. Imagine you are at a job interview, why should the interviewer hire you?

You are the Expert

There is more to networking than just meeting

Your Notes and Thoughts

people. You must give those you network with a reason to remember you. You must stand out from the crowd. You know more about your own business than anyone else, so you ARE the expert.

> **Here's a tip:** Write an OpEd or an article for publication regarding your field of expertise

Put all doubts out of your mind.

Need an icebreaker?

When you're in a business networking situation, having introduced yourself to another guest, it's not always easy to come up with that question that's going to get you into the conversation, intelligently, and with your self-esteem intact!
Here are a few you could try:
- How did you get started in your business?
- What do you love most about your profession?
- Why is your company better than your competitors?
- If someone were to consider a career in your field, what advice would you give them?
- What is the one thing you would do with your business if you knew you would not fail?
- How do you see your industry has changed through the years?
- Do you see any coming trends in your business?
- What is the strangest or funniest thing you have experienced in your business?

Your Notes and Thoughts

- What do you consider the best way you've found to promote your business?
- How would you like people to describe your business?

Of course you should use language that is comfortable to you, and only use questions that resonate with you.

Your Notes and Thoughts

Bonus Chapter Networking 1-on-1 for senior citizens

When my mother was in her eighties, she started to fall more often. She would forget to turn off the stove, and many other "little" things that could potentially add up to one big disaster.

My sister and I made the decision that it was not safe for her to live alone any more, and that the best place for her would be in a nursing home. She would have qualified caregivers available to her, and if an accident should happen then she would be in the right spot.

She went to the nursing home – incidentally, called The Beverly Home - kicking and screaming. She accused my sister and I of putting her in there to die, she said we were sending her to jail, and many other awful things that we never expected to hear from our mother!

Within two weeks she was calling bingo games! Not just playing bingo, but actually calling the numbers. She was participating in every activity she possibly could, and was even helping to take care of some of the other residents.

Why is networking important to nursing home residents?

Many elderly people who are "sent" to nursing

Your Notes and Thoughts

homes by their families complain that "they've put me here to die" – and of course that's true, but you have to die somewhere!

If our parents and grandparents go into these residential facilities with that attitude, and are never taught how to interact with other residents, these feelings of abandonment can overwhelm, and the elder becomes withdrawn and non-participatory. They feel abandoned, and start to feel self-pity, and it becomes a vicious circle.

It may seem that attempts to involve them in activities are merely gratuitous, and are therefore resented. It may seem to the family that they are just not interested in participating, without realizing there could be an element of fear involved.

Sometimes we do not realize that we need to re-teach our elders the "art" of introducing themselves to others, methods of integrating themselves into group situations, and how to "play nice" with other residents. If they have been used to being in their own home, either alone or with a partner, it is very likely that they haven't been interacting with others their own age, and just don't know how to break the ice.

If you have a loved one in this situation, there are many ideas you can give them to help ease them back into the "mingling" mindset.

Your Notes and Thoughts

For instance, if you see a card game in action and there's an empty seat, a simple "do you mind if I join you?" could get you in the game! The same is true in the dining room. If you see someone dining alone, they may be in the same position as you. They could be unsure how to start up a conversation with someone. Introduce yourself! "Hi, I'm Bev, is someone joining you, or do you mind if I sit here?"

It does take courage to make the first move, however, if you've read some of the tips and tricks of business networking, you can just apply them to this nursing home situation!

If there are no clubs or groups your elder relates to, have them start one. It could be a craft group, such as knitting, sewing, woodworking, etc., or a game group, such a board games, card games, and such.

They should be encouraged to participate in events organized by the home. Maybe they attend concerts or go on day trips. There may be visitors such as pastors, or people who can teach a craft or hobby. These are excellent opportunities to buddy up with another resident!

Seminars

Networking 1-on-1's primary goal is to network with individuals on a one on one basis to discover their needs, their fears, and what they need to do to be

Your Notes and Thoughts

successful.

However, another helpful tool can be a seminar. This is useful to a small group by identifying some of the areas that are most important in the networking arena. It is not directed toward any individual in the room, but each person can learn many new tools during a presentation.

Seminars are not for everyone, but they could benefit everyone when they later realize how much they can accomplish from a one on one session.

Of the principles outlined in the seminar, there will always be certain ideas that each person could find helpful and could implement in a one on one discussion.

Question and answer times in a seminar can also give the other parties in the room a different perspective on networking. Each individual has their own idea of what constitutes successful networking, and by asking questions they can bring up their own personal concerns that could spark a solution for another attendee.

One should not limit oneself in the pursuit of networking knowledge by just participating in one area. The one on one, seminars, and other avenues can all be useful. Therefore, it is best not to limit oneself to one specific networking method.

Your Notes and Thoughts

Networking in alternative situations

I recently had the opportunity to visit a women's prison, with the intention of passing along some networking knowledge to about 100 of the inmates.

Having an incarceration on your record is a huge barrier to overcome in many situations, so some extra networking skills could help these women to better integrate when they return to civilian life.

The advice I gave them for their "life on the inside" was to make the best of the situation they are in by focusing on the following:

- Take any classes that are offered
- Use all recreational opportunities
- Befriend each other
- Prepare for when they are released
- Plan for their future
- Keep a positive attitude
- Be loving of others
- Make yourself a person people can rely on
- Encourage each other

By following some, or all, of these tips, inmates can help to prepare for life after release and look forward to a more positive future.

I was so thankful for the opportunity to present potential lifestyle changes to these young ladies, I must say it was extremely exciting and fulfilling for me.

Your Notes and Thoughts

Networking Tools

Business Cards

One of the most critical tools of your business is your business card. It lingers longer than you can imagine. People seem to think it's groovy to make an ornate design, using logos, on their business cards. It IS a good idea to utilize your logo to some degree on your business card as it makes you more recognizable.

However, when designing your business cards, you need to consider several elements. The name of your business should be prominent, bold and very legible.

Applications that can scan business cards into a mobile phone content management system are very popular. If the background of your card is dark, or has a "busy" pattern, it is hard for the scan to pick up the essential information. Keep your design simple!

Your name should also be legible, but maybe not as large as the business name. Your business address is an important part of your contact information and should be on your business card. However; never, **never** put your personal home address on your business card! If you own a home based business, you can use a Post Office mailbox address, or just the city and State, but never your street address!

Your Notes and Thoughts

The important contact information is your cell phone number, email, and webpage. It is just as important that a person can read this quickly, and without the use of a magnifying glass!

If one feels it necessary to add some of the products or services the business offers, that information belongs on the back of the card. Then you do not distract from the important information on the front of the card.

Print and Vehicle Advertising

Likewise, print advertising and the ever-popular vehicle advertising, need to send the same message.

There are many kinds of advertising signs you can use on your company vehicle. Before you commit to a final version, it is good practice to mock up the signage on paper in the size you intend to use, tape it to the vehicle in the desired position, and have someone drive your vehicle by. If you can read it from a distance of approximately 20 feet, you're ready for the final, permanent signage.

Some vehicles are wrapped, or partially wrapped, with colorful designs. As long as you stay with the theme of your business, and the graphics being legible – especially a highly visible phone number – this is a very good and cost effective advertising medium.

Your Notes and Thoughts

Billboards

While on the theme of advertising, electronic billboards are very popular. Your contract will specify how often your advertisement will show, and it will be up for 8-10 seconds.

This form of advertising does have its drawbacks. As with any form of promotion, visibility is the key. Of course, location, location, location is your first concern. There are a few electronic billboards that were placed in great locations, and within a year a tree grew and obscured them.

Be aware of some of the potential drawbacks before contracting to place a billboard!
You can design your own ad, or have the billboard company assist you, but keep your design simple and crisp, and your information LARGE and legible!

Your Notes and Thoughts

Testimonials

Robert McBeath

The years have come and gone, over fifteen in fact, and my relationship with Robert McBeath has grown. In this time, he has also grown his business, and in his personal life. He is married now, with a beautiful wife. His career has blossomed, and he and his wife have won many awards for their business ventures.

I have always felt that Robert has been as helpful to me as I have been to him.

He rose from a shy young man who walked into Business After Hours, to a successful businessman with lots of confidence in himself, and in his business.

"I remember when I was new to Bloomington, back in 1996. Also new to business, I heard about the local chamber of commerce and despite my nerves about being alone, new and an outsider, I ventured into my first after hours event.

I remember stepping through the door, looking at a mass of strangers and feeling like I didn't belong. As I stood there fighting a panic attack, I was debating whether to find a corner or just bolt. That's exactly the point where Bev Edgerton walked up to me and warmly introduced

Your Notes and Thoughts

herself. She not only made me feel comfortable with her, she proceeded to walk me around the room, make small talk and introduce me to many other influential people that night. That is only the beginning of what she's done for me over the years.

Thanks to her coaching and encouragement, I feel like a fixture in the community. I give her full credit for my all my involvement in the McLean Chamber of Commerce as well as winning the Chamber of Commerce Presidents Award in 2002! To say she's had a major impact on the success of my career would be putting it mildly.

What's even more incredible is that my story isn't isolated. She has had that very same impact on hundreds of individuals through the years and, to this day, at any networking event you'll find her going out of her way to make everyone feel welcome.

I'm so proud to call Bev Edgerton an associate and count her among my closest of friends."

Robert McBeath, President
Cornerstone Business Solutions

Your Notes and Thoughts

Melissa Lockwood

One great privilege I had was to meet Dr. Melissa Lockwood, as she had just come into our area to practice as a podiatrist. Her smile and the encouragement she received from her husband have been such an asset to her practice.

She has grown and become a well-recognized physician in the Bloomington-Normal area, and serves her community by going to nursing homes to assist residents with their podiatry needs.

"Bev is a true 'mover and shaker' here in McLean County!! After meeting her through the McLean County Chamber of Commerce, she introduced me to so many people - business owners, fellow physicians, ALL potential patients.

Through her networking meet and greets, I gained confidence in speaking with other community leaders and learning more about the potential market as a new provider. She is A+ at getting YOU connected and her recommendations go far in enhancing your business!!"

Melissa Lockwood, DPM
Heartland Foot and Ankle Associates, P.C.

Your Notes and Thoughts

Keith Laible

When I met Keith, I would not have expected he needed any one-on-one training from me. He was extremely outgoing, personable and an excellent salesman, but he wanted to know more about networking in certain situations, especially Chamber events and other social situations.

It was really my pleasure to have worked with him, and to know that he feels I was a help to him.

"I recommend Bev Edgerton's Networking One-on-One to anyone who wants to learn certain things that will give you the confidence to meet and greet people. If you are shy and get nervous when out with the public, Bev can teach you how to attend gatherings by using the skills she herself uses. Call Bev and get your session scheduled. It truly will make you a different person."

Keith Laible
Print/Mail Solutions Provider
Your Vision + Wayne Printing

Your Notes and Thoughts

Belinda T

I first met Belinda in my other life as a Realtor. She has a warm personality that is very conducive to forming friendships.

I knew she would be successful!

She attended a seminar I gave, and to my surprise, she wrote four full pages as I talked. She felt it really enhanced her career and knowledge of networking and made me feel very good!

"One of Beverly's many gifts is the ability to love, and to encourage and exhort others.

As my mentor for over eight years, I have the benefit of gaining first-hand knowledge from her. I attended one of her One-on-One Networking Sessions and, four pages of notes later, I was amazed at the wisdom that she imparted!

Beverly has the ability to cause her audience to think, and leaves them excitedly wanting more! This book is a great investment to motivate you to believe in yourself again."

Belinda T

Your Notes and Thoughts

Willonda Herrod

Having met this young lady through the Chamber, we were instant friends! Her job entails meeting a lot of people, and she felt she would like to sit down at the job with more networking experience.

We had a very productive session. Shortly after that, I had planned to meet her at an After Hours social. When she came in, we talked for a few minutes and then I lost track of her.

Believing she was my responsibility, I immediately began to search for her in every corner. I just knew she would be standing in a corner somewhere, waiting for me. When I found her, she was standing at a table, having a snack. I approached her and apologized, "I've lost track of you, are you OK?" She held up a handful of business cards and said, "I've been doing what you've told me – I went and gave all these people my cards, and got theirs. Isn't that what I was supposed to be doing?" I will never doubt her again!

"I worked with Beverly Edgerton and she really taught me a lot about social networking and the benefits of doing certain things such as reading the newspaper and etiquette when approaching people.

I have to say that by taking the Networking 1-on-1 class with Bev it has enabled me to feel more

Your Notes and Thoughts

confident when at social networking events and it has enhanced my business opportunities.

Bev is amazing and Networking 1-on-1 is the real thing."

Willonda Herrod

Your Notes and Thoughts

Darryl Brown

Darryl has succeeded in many different facets of the banking business, and continues to do so. He called me to ask if he could meet me for a while, before I had Networking 1-on-1. I figured he was trying to sell me something, right?

Wrong!

Darryl's first words were "I want to know everything you know about networking. I want you to pour everything you know into me." I must say, I was astonished at the time that anyone would think I knew everything there is to know about networking.

However, a few years later, Darryl invited me to one of his new offices to show it off. We spent an hour or so talking. He then said, "Why don't you start a business?" and I asked why. He said, "Why don't you start a business to teach people how to network?"

We worked on the details, and the rest is history!

"If you are looking for someone to show you how to specifically connect with people, give Bev a try. You cannot lose...she will make sure of it. Bev will not only tell you what to do, she will show you how to do it. She doesn't guarantee sales she guarantees confidence.

Your Notes and Thoughts

No one can sell your business like you can. As business owners, what we often lack in the selling process is the confidence to get the sales conversation started. Bev's presence alone will boost your confidence to be able to present yourself and business in a way that makes you proud to own your business."

Darryl L. Brown
Assistant Vice President - Business Banking
PNC Bank

Your Notes and Thoughts

The ideas shared in this book are just a starting point. You can schedule your very own one-on-one session with Bev and discover techniques that are applicable to your personal situation or networking style.

Bev Edgerton has excelled in the business world for over 19 years. Her motto, "You are my most important client" is evidenced in her exemplary service. Her versatility, flexibility and availability combined with awareness of the ever-changing market are a rare combination.

Other business related positions gave her the opportunity to cultivate the skills of service, detail, and caring.

Bev firmly believes that "giving back" builds a strong community. She is constantly building bridges and connecting people wherever she goes. For those who know her, Bev's spirit of giving makes her a true gift, indeed.

She has volunteered with the McLean County Historical Society, the Humane Society, Easter Seals, United Way, Downtown Bloomington Association, Muscular Dystrophy Association, and the Alzheimer's Association.

Bev has received many awards and recognitions for her public service through the Chamber of Commerce, BNI, the Bloomington Normal Association of Realtors, and other related organizations.

Your Notes and Thoughts

Bev is happy to be invited to speak at seminars, at retirement facilities, correctional institutions, or at educational meetings.

The possibilities are endless when you consider that everyone in the community can benefit from some networking knowledge!

Do you struggle with:
- Forgetting your business cards?
- Being unprepared?
- Unfamiliar with the event?
- Over/Under-dressing?
- Shyness or boldness?
- Where to network for your specific business or particular area of expertise?

Bev has a special offer for you. Contact The Edge at bevedge@aol.com and mention you've invested in this book, to get your special rate.

Expand your networking horizons with Networking 1-on-1.

Your Notes and Thoughts